Loughb

on old pictui .

Dave Dover

1. The publisher of this multiview card managed to transpose the captions of the Town Hall and Carnegie Library. The "Bull's Head" on High Street is featured prominently on the picture bottom right.

£2.95

**Designed and Published by
Reflections of a Bygone Age,
Keyworth, Nottingham**

1992

All rights reserved. No part of this book may be reproduced or transmitted in any form or by any means, electronic or mechanical, including photocopying, recording or by any information storage and retrieval system, without permission in writing from the Publisher.

**Printed by
Adlard Print and Typesetting Services,
Ruddington, Notts.**

ISBN 0 946245 55 X

Loughborough is a town with an ever-changing face. The old and the new can be only properly appreciated when seen in photographs or postcards, and I've tried in this book to represent the changes that have occurred, and the images that remain. Those old enough to remember will be able to recognise familiar landmarks, while younger people may look in amazement.

Front cover: 'Peveril' series postcard featuring five views of Loughborough, and posted to Skegness in September 1920. Note the view of Mill Street (top left), now Market Street.

Back cover (top): A marvellously animated Swan Street about 1908 on a 'Peveril' series card.

(bottom): Loughborough Parish Church looking from Rectory Place down New Road. The houses in the distance are on Church Gate.

Queen's Park, Loughborough.   *Peveril Series.*

2. An early 'Peveril' series card showing the bandstand in Queens Park. *"We have had many a happy hour here,"* wrote the sender when this was posted in September 1904.

CARNEGIE LIBRARY FROM PARK. LOUGHBORO.

3. The Carnegie Library (centre) was opened in 1905 by Joseph Griggs, former mayor of Loughborough. This photographic card by anonymous publisher shows the view from Queens Park with the public memorial baths on the left and footbridge over the lake.

INTRODUCTION

Until 1888, Loughborough was mainly a small market town with Knight Thorpe, Thorpe Acre and Garenden little surrounding hamlets. When the municipal borough was formed, major developments lay ahead. The construction of the sewage works and purchase of the gas works co-incided with the arrival of the Brush works and Herbert Morris Ltd. These developments, and the founding of Loughborough College early this century, stimulated the prosperity of the town, which began to spread, absorbing the hamlets. The town centre itself has undergone many changes, and is still doing so. Today, the outskirts of the town are altering, with green belt being eaten away by housing and industrial development, along with new roads. Loughborough still holds a great deal of the past, yet is eagerly looking to the future.

Dave Dover
September 1992

This book sets out to portray Loughborough as it was earlier this century through the medium of picture postcards. These were first published in Britain in 1894, but it was not until a decade later that they began to take off, when in 1902 the Post Office allowed a message to be written on the address side. This meant that the whole of one side was available for the picture and obviously gave more scope to publishers. Photographic viewcards became very popular, and the postcard became the most important way of communicating news or messages, in much the same way as the telephone is used today. The years up to 1914 were the 'Golden Age' of picture postcards, when millions of imaginative designs covering every subject under the sun were published by a host of national and local firms. There's hardly a village or hamlet that wasn't documented at that time by a postcard publisher, though sometimes the number of cards available was unrelated to the size of a community.

The postcards in this book are the work of seventeen named publishers, though some were produced anonymously. Most of these were national or out-of-town firms, for Loughborough had a large enough population to make it worthwhile for these bigger concerns to interest themselves in the town. There was no local publisher who established himself as an important issuer of postcards, though several are represented in here with the odd card.

4. Ashby Road looking away from the town centre. Little has changed as far as the houses are concerned, though noteworthy on this 'Peveril' series postcard is the total absence of traffic: A young boy is casually walking his dog in the middle of the road! *"I am at Ansty for the weekend, just going to Bradgate",* wrote Edie to Ada on a card posted at Anstey in August 1912.

5. A rural Ashby Road half a mile out of town on a c.1930 postcard *"The sheep arrived this morning at eleven o'clock."*

"COTES" MILL, LOUGHBOROUGH

S 2359

6. Cotes Mill on a W.H. Smith 'Kingsway' series postcard sent from Loughborough in October 1908. The gentleman in the picture is possibly one of the mill's new owners, Goodacre or Everard. This was still a working mill until 1973, but is now a public house.

FLOODED MILL
LOUGHBOROUGH

7. The River Soar has always been prone to flooding, and dating this postcard is not easy, though it appears to be early 1920s. *"I am stopping at school till I am fifteen"*, wrote Everard (son of the owner) *"for I have got a scholarship when I was twelve for three years."*

Church Gate, Loughborough.

Peveril Series.

8. Church Gate is one of the few streets in Loughborough left almost intact, with many of the shopfronts still as they are in this postcard in the 'Peveril' series, posted to Plumtree in December 1904.

THE NOTION SHOP   THE NOTION SHOP   THE NOTION SHOP

47 C. D & E CHURCHGATE, LOUGHBOROUGH

9. "The Notion Shop", a draper's at 47 Church Gate, on an early postcard. The frontage is still the same today.

E 38071

Swa

10. Swan Street on a card by O.F. Stengel of London, posted to Skipton in August 1916. A large crowd have obligingly posed for the photographer. This street was included in the widening scheme in the 1920s *(compare illus. 13).*

eet, Loughborough.

11. Another Church Gate shop, belonging to Robert Ball, with the proud owner standing outside his shop. A superb window display of goods is evident. Postcard by the Midland Photo Co. of Loughborough.

12. Swan Street during the 1930s on a card by Valentine of Dundee. The *Loughborough Echo* building is prominent on the left, with the Newman & Skinner premises further on. Note the period pram outside A. Ives' shoe shop.

LBH 1   SWAN STREET, LOUGHBOROUGH   A TUCK CARD

13. A 1950s Raphael Tuck postcard of Swan Street with again very little traffic in evidence. On this view from Market Place, the Benefit shoe shop is on the right, and the "Green Man" Hotel in the centre distance. Other shops/premises in Swan Street at this time included T. Barker & Son (builders), Baum (florist), Cockerill (grocer), Coleman (outfitter), Creamline Taxi Co., Curry's, E. Kirke (confectioner), W. Palfreman, A. Prince (garage), H. Prince (sports outfitter), E. Rook (jeweller), E.W. Simpson (butcher), and W.H. Smith.

14. Loughborough Parish Church, the highest point in the town. This 'Rex' series postcard is of c.1924 vintage. *(see also back cover illus.)*

GRANBY STREET, LOUGHBOROUGH

15. Granby Street in the 1930s, with the Carnegie Library on the right. This view is taken from the direction of the Cattle Market. Card published by the Echo Press, Loughborough.

THE CEMETERY, LOUGHBOROUGH.

16. The cemetery gates, Leicester Road, on a postcard by John E. Lee, bookseller and stationer, posted from the town in March 1908. *"This is one of the prettiest places we can boast of, rather different to Mansfield,"* wrote Nellie to Miss Edge.

Leicester Road, Loughborough

17. Leicester Road at the junction with Beeches Road in the 1930s. A garage still stands at the same spot on the right today.

18. Leicester Road looking up from the High Street. The 'Home Cafe' is at no. 22 on the right, with Chamberlains, motor engineers, next door. 'Rex' series card of the early 1920s.

Leicester Road, Loughborough

19. A card of Leicester Road looking towards the town centre. On the right is the "Royal Oak" public house. Card posted to Horncastle in October 1911.

20. The Wesleyan Methodist Church on Leicester Road, no longer used for its original purpose but still standing today. Photographic card of about 1906. At one time it was an army surplus store but is now empty.

21. *"I think they have made it look better than it is,"* observed the writer of this postcard sent to the County Asylum at Stafford in April 1906. It was published by Thos. Gillott of Loughborough and shows Toothill Road.

LGH.35.   ALAN MOSS ROAD, LOUGHBOROUGH   Copyright
Frith Ltd.

22. Alan Moss Road looking from the Derby Road direction on a late 1950s postcard by Francis Frith of Reigate. This was one of the many out-of-town housing developments, built in 1949-50.

THE CARILLON
WAR MEMORIAL, LOUGHBOROUGH
Opened July 22nd. 1923

23. Loughborough's Carillon, the war memorial, was opened on 22nd July 1923 in Queen's Park. Its height is 153 feet.

24. The "Bull's Head" on Shelthorpe Road. In the background are shops built for the 1930s estate.

25. Shelthorpe School on another card by the same — but anonymous — publisher.

26. The Loughborough fire brigade turning out of the fire s
the technical college. The men in this picture could well ha
lus. 28). Postcard by Pallett & Co., Loughborough, publish

on Ashby Road next to the town offices, later to become
ended the fire at Loughborough Day School in 1903 *(see il-*
bout 1906.

27. Loughborough Technical College in the early 1920s on 'Rex' series postcard no. 670. Adverts under the clock announce a garden fete on June 1st (to be opened by Countess Ferrers) and the annual sports on Saturday, June 18th. The college building, on the corner of Ashby Road and Greenclose Lane, was originally built in 1877 as municipal offices and a small library. It became the college in 1909. The site today is Sainsbury's food store.

Photo by J. H. Wilson, Leicester.

Fire at Loughborough Day School.

28. Fire at Loughborough Day School in Churchgate in 1903 on a postcard by J.H. Wilson of Leicester.

Bedford Square, Loughborough   PN4562

29. Bedford Square looking across towards Queens Park and the Carillon on a 1950s photographic postcard. Bramley's fruit shop is on the corner and the "Wheatsheaf Hotel" to the right, run at this time by Mr H. James.

GRAMMAR SCHOOL, LOUGHBOROUGH.   92738.

30. Loughborough Grammar School, built in 1852, on a 1920s Valentine postcard.

NOTTINGHAM ROAD. LOUGHBOROUGH.

31. Nottingham Road looking towards the Midland railway station (on the left) at what is now a busy traffic light-controlled junction. This 'Peveril' series card was posted at Coventry in February 1918.

PEVERIL REAL PHOTO SERIES.   NOTTINGHAM ROAD. LOUGHBOROUGH. SHOWING TOWLE'S FACTORY.

32. Towle's factory on the corner of Nottingham Road and Clarence Street, with a milkman on his delivery round at the left. This building is still standing today. 'Peveril' card of the 1920s.

33. W.H. Smith postcard of Frederick Street, with Harry and Alice sending it to indicate where their house is at no. 67. This picture dates from c.1910.

34. The canal bank looking away from Bridge Street on a Valentine's postcard of about 1910.

Burleigh Brook Park, Loughborough.

35. Burleigh Brook Park, just outside the built-up area along Ashby Road and near where Cotswold Close is today, was a boating lake and popular venue for school trips. The card, by London publishers Hartmann, was sent from Nuneaton in February 1909.

KING ST AND GREAT CENTRAL HOTEL. LOUGHBORO'

36. The Great Central Hotel on King Street is featured on a card posted at Nottingham in October 1905. The G.C. railway station, sited behind the camera's vantage point, is an elusive location as far as postcards are concerned — along with the Midland station. It has survived closure, though, and re-emerged as a thriving preserved steam railway.

S 2360   THE BRUSH WORKS, LOUGHBOROUGH.

37. The Brush works on Nottingham Road seen on a W.H. Smith 'Kingsway' series card postally used in March 1909. The company first traded as Henry Hughes & Co. in 1865, before becoming Falcon Engineering and Car Works. Their main products have been light railway cars, trams, steam locomotives and, later, diesel electric units.

PARK RD
LOUGHBOROUGH

38. Park Road in 1908 on a photographic card published by W. Draper of Loughborough. These houses are still standing today.

39. The Convent School on Park Road in 1906. This scene is still with us apart from the gas lamp on the left.

40. Burton Street is also little changed today, though there are likely to be rather more motor cars than on this 1910 postcard.

BEACON ROAD, LOUGHBOROUGH.

261

41. Beacon Road in 1914 on a W.H. Smith card. The writer mentions having been on *"a ride on my bicycle tonight"*.

42. Park Street and the corner of Grey Street. This postcard was sent from the town in May 1905.

The Green Man Hotel, Loughborough.

43. The "Green Man" Hotel on Swan Street; this is no longer standing (it was demolished in 1971), but the name carries on as a cellar bar.

44. Loughborough Cattle Market in 1917. The building in the centre is now the National Westminster Bank.

45. Market Street looking from the top of the Market Place in the 1950s. Shops in the street at this time included Aileen (hairdresser), Ainley & Bleackley (baby linen), Barker (baker), Diss & Sons (leather goods), Gaskill (stationer), Willett & Mark (jewellers), Pennington (auctioneers) and Stokes (gents outfitters).

TOWN HALL, LOUGHBOROUGH.

46. The impressive facade of the Town Hall in 1908 with the "Lord Nelson" Inn in the middle distance. This card was published by Boots Cash Chemists.

Market Place, Loughborough.

47. A virtually deserted Market Place on another Boots postcard sent from Loughborough in July 1905. Boots' own shop is on the right, with the "Lord Nelson" to the left and the Town Hall in the distance.

E 38063

Market Place, Loughborough.

48. A much livelier scene about 1907, giving a wider view of Market Place. Waterloo House is on the right and Tom Cann's boot and shoe shop in the centre distance. Card published by Stengel of London.

MARKET PLACE, LOUGHBOROUGH

49. The market stalls are featured on this Valentine's card postally used in 1916. Bailey and Simpkin's shop is on the right.

Market Place, Loughborough   PN4557

50. An interesting selection of motor vehicles on this 1960s view of Market Place looking towards High Street and Biggin Street.

High Street, Loughborough.

51. An early Boots postcard of High Street, posted from Loughborough in March 1905. Again, it is the narrowness of the street which is particularly striking.

Market Place, Loughborough   PN1345

52. High Street at the junction with Baxter Gate, looking towards Swan Street and Biggin Street on a 1950s postcard. Traffic is also coming from the Market Place.

High Street, Loughborough.

53. High Street looking towards the Market Place, again in the 1950s, with the "Black Bull" on the left. Card published by Co-operative Stationery, Market Place.

54. Baxter Gate about 1905, well before road widening took place, on a Stengel postcard. The "Rose and Crown" (proprietor Sam Cook) is on the left.

55. Baxter Gate in the 1950s, featured on a Frith postcard. The road was widened in the mid-1920s.

LBH 16　　　　　　　FOREST ROAD, LOUGHBOROUGH　　　　　　A TUCK CARD

56. Forest Road looking from where the Epinal Way roundabout is today. Raphael Tuck card, posted at Leicester in July 1956.

Trinity Church　　　　　　　　　　Loughborough

57. Trinity Church on Moor Lane. This c.1905 postcard was published by John Corah & Son, 20 High Street, Loughborough.